The Dinosaurs
and the Dark Star

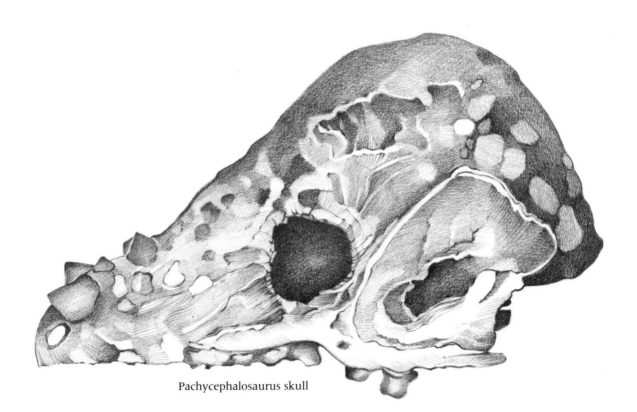

Pachycephalosaurus skull

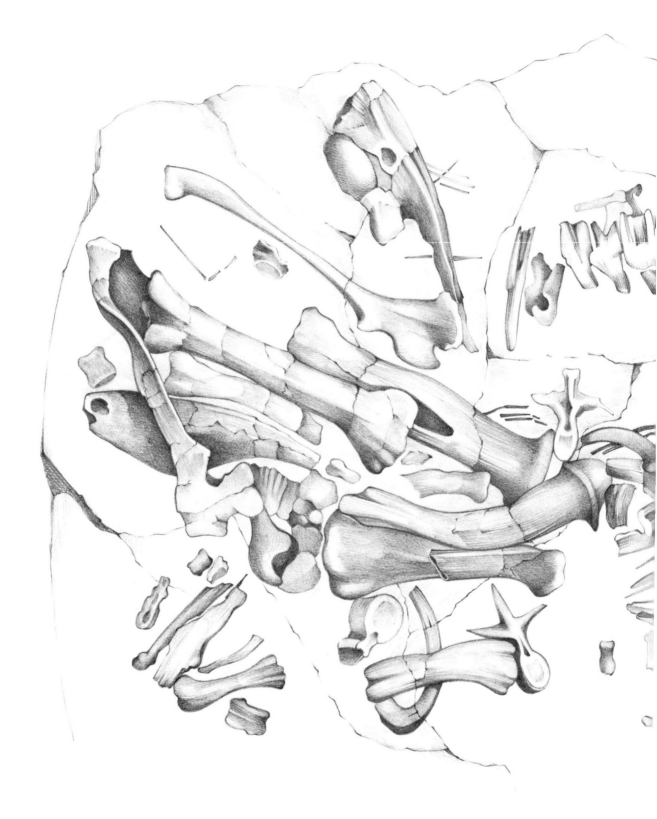

The Dinosaurs and the Dark Star

BY ROBIN BATES
AND CHERYL SIMON

ILLUSTRATED BY
JENNIFER DEWEY

MACMILLAN PUBLISHING COMPANY/New York
COLLIER MACMILLAN PUBLISHERS/London

Macmillan books are available at special discounts
for bulk purchases for sales promotions, premiums,
fund raising, or educational use. Special editions
or book excerpts can also be created to specifica-
tion. For details, contact:
    Special Sales Director
    Macmillan Publishing Company
    866 Third Avenue
    New York, N.Y. 10022

Macmillan Publishing Company
866 Third Avenue, New York, N.Y. 10022
Collier Macmillan Canada, Inc.
Printed in the United States of America
10 9 8 7 6 5 4 3 2
Library of Congress Cataloging in Publication Data
Bates, Robin, date.
  The dinosaurs and the dark star.
  Includes index.
  Summary: Discusses the methods used by scientists of
the last two centuries to interpret the fossil evidence
of dinosaurs, and explores theories as to why they became
extinct.
    1. Dinosaurs—Juvenile literature. 2. Planets, Minor—
Juvenile literature. [1. Dinosaurs. 2. Planets, Minor.
3. Paleontology] I. Simon, Cheryl. II. Dewey, Jennifer,
ill. III. Title.
QE862.D5B38 1985   567.9'1   84-3922
ISBN 0-02-708340-3

To my parents—*R.B.*
To my parents—*C.S.*
For Phelps—*J.D.*

Stegosaurus

Contents

Introduction

Millions of years ago, strange monsters ruled the earth. There were no people then, or televisions or schools or cars. But the monsters, called dinosaurs, found plenty to keep them busy. Not only did they have to spend a lot of time searching for food, but they also had to watch out for other dinosaurs that wanted to attack them. The world was a dangerous place.

Let's imagine that one day *Tyrannosaurus*, one of the fiercest dinosaurs, hid quietly in the trees, waiting for another dinosaur to walk by. *Tyrannosaurus* had not eaten for several days. It was a big, clumsy monster and could not walk as fast as some of the other dinosaurs, so it waited. Then, *Triceratops* approached. It looked like a giant rhinoceros, with three sharp horns and a bony shield over its neck. With a roar, *Tyrannosaurus* lunged and sank its knifelike teeth into *Triceratops*'s leathery skin. *Triceratops* fought valiantly, but soon fell to its knees and, with a long sigh, was dead. *Tyrannosaurus* settled down to eat, ripping off huge chunks of flesh and swallowing them whole. For the tyrannosaur, it was just an ordinary day.

But out in space, something out of the ordinary was happening. A comet, with a gleaming head and glistening tail, was heading for the earth. For the dinosaurs, nothing appeared unusual, for at that time, the whole heavens were filled with comets—shining swords in the night sky. For thousands of years, ever since any of the dinosaurs then living could remember, the sky had been this way—a greater fireworks display than any Fourth of July. These comets often passed the earth, but never, in the dinosaurs' history, had one come so close.

9   *Tyrannosaurus* looked up from its dinner and stared at the strange sight in the sky. Hundreds of miles away, the comet struck the earth in a blinding flash. The ground shook beneath the dinosaur's clawed feet as the shock waves spread, the way ripples move out in circles when a pebble is thrown into a pond. The shaking of the earth scared even the tyrannosaur. It abandoned its prey and hurried off to the nearest thicket to hide.

The comet's impact created a gaping hole in the earth—a gigantic crater, five miles deep and one hundred miles wide. Millions of tons of rock and dust were blasted into the sky. A thick cloud swept swiftly over the earth, blocking out the sun. For months, night replaced day. Without the sun's warmth, the earth began to freeze. Finally, when the clouds rolled away, all the dinosaurs were gone. Silence was everywhere. The earth must have been a lonely place.

No one knows if the story you have just read is true. But it is the latest idea of scientists who are trying to solve one of the great mysteries of our world. For 140 million years, dinosaurs ruled the earth. Then, 65 million years ago, they disappeared. The sky also was empty: The pterosaurs, flying reptiles larger than the largest bird, were gone. All the giant animals that lived in the waters, like the long-necked ple-siosaurs and the mosasaurs—swimming lizards with flat, snaky tails and paddlelike feet—vanished, too. Millions of other swimming creatures, so tiny that they would be hard to see with the naked eye, also disappeared.

When many kinds of life die at one time, scientists call it a mass extinction. This was one of the biggest mass extinctions since the earth was formed. Altogether, nearly three-quarters of the kinds of animal and plant species then living died along with the dinosaurs.

This book is a story of discovery. It is about how dinosaurs were found and about the people who found them. It is about what dinosaurs were like and about why they disappeared.

It is also about a thin layer of clay that for millions of years lay unnoticed beneath our feet. To everyone's surprise, it has led to the suggestion that there is a mysterious dark star nearby—a companion to our sun. It's an exciting tale. A good place to begin is with the clay layer and how it came to be linked with all the death and destruction.

Pteranodon

The Clue in the Clay

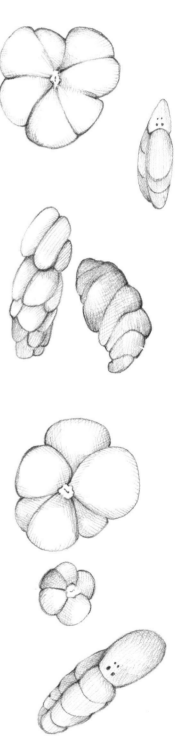

In 1978 Walter Alvarez, a professor of geology from Berkeley, California, paid his usual summer visit to the little medieval town of Gubbio in central Italy. He went there to continue his study of the rocks in a deep limestone gorge behind the town.

The limestone had formed while the dinosaurs were living, when the sea covered that part of the earth. At that time, millions of tiny animals called forams lived in the seas, feeding on algae and bacteria even smaller than they themselves. When the forams died, their hard, chalky shells drifted to the sea floor. They piled up, one on top of another, gradually becoming layers of limestone. The layering happened very slowly: It had taken 80 million years to build the rock in the gorge.

One day, as Walter Alvarez drove along the twisting road that led through the gorge, he happened to gaze at the cliffs towering over him on either side. Originally the layers of limestone had been laid down flat. Over millions of years, forces inside the earth had pushed them upward until now they were tilted up at a forty-five-degree angle. The layers that Walter passed close to the town were the oldest; farther up the gorge, they were much younger. It was rather like driving through time.

Toward the end of the gorge Walter stopped his car and climbed out. Taking his magnifying glass, he examined the rock closely. For hundreds of yards on either side the limestone was full of dozens of different forams. But just at this point, where the rocks were 65 million years old, there were almost none. The great variety of shells ceased, and the next

11

rock layer held only forams of a single kind. Walter knew that something similar occurred in rocks containing dinosaur bones. At the same point in time all their bones disappeared and no further traces of the giant animals could be found.

As Walter studied the rock, he noticed something very odd. A thin layer of clay ran through it, just where the forams disappeared. It was as if a faint gray line had been drawn through the earth, marking the end of one era and the start of the next. Walter had no idea what it was doing in the middle of the limestone. Somehow, he sensed it was important. Chipping a piece off, he put it safely away.

When he got back to California, Walter showed the clay layer to his father, Luis. Luis Alvarez is a famous physicist who received the Nobel Prize in 1968 for his work on atoms. He did not know much about rocks, but he liked puzzles, and he was very puzzled by the layer of clay. To satisfy his curiosity, he decided to find out why the clay was there.

First of all, he told Walter, they should figure out how long the clay had taken to form. He quickly thought up a clever way of doing this—by measuring how much cosmic dust was in the clay. Luis knew that space around the earth is not really empty. It is full of dust. Although it is too fine for us to see, one hundred thousand tons of it are swept up by the earth each year on its journey around the sun.

A lot of dust would have fallen into the clay if it had taken a long time to form. If the clay had built up more quickly, it would contain less dust. Luis decided that the amount of dust could be measured, since it contained an unusual metal called iridium. He asked two of his colleagues, Frank Asaro and Helen Michel, to help with the difficult task of measuring the iridium. It would be present in very tiny amounts, mixed up with the thirty or so other elements in the clay.

Frank and Helen set to work. They took minute samples of the clay to the nuclear reactor at Berkeley and bombarded

13 them with neutrons, one of the kinds of particles from which atoms are made. The neutrons excited the atoms in the clay, so that they gave off little bursts of energy called gamma rays. The pattern of rays told Frank and Helen which elements and how much of them the clay contained. Within a few weeks they had the answer. It astonished everyone. The clay did contain iridium, but in huge amounts. There was far more than could have come from the cosmic dust alone.

Luis was more puzzled than ever. He had started with one question—How long did the clay take to form?—and ended up with another: Why did it contain so *much* iridium? He spent the next few weeks thinking hard. Whenever he had a new idea, he would discuss it with Frank and Helen. Each time, one of them found a reason why it would not work. Finally, he found an explanation that none of them could prove was wrong. It was, perhaps, the most exciting of all the ideas he had had.

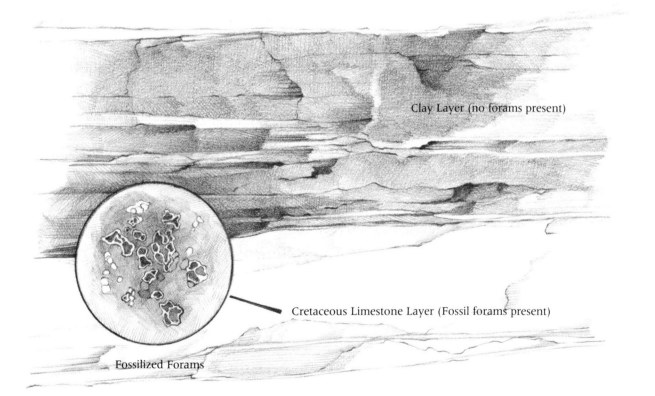

Clay Layer (no forams present)

Cretaceous Limestone Layer (Fossil forams present)

Fossilized Forams

14 Luis suggested that a large asteroid or a comet had crashed into the earth. Asteroids are small, rocky bodies, tiny planets a few yards to several miles across, that circle the sun. Thousands of asteroids fly through space in the Asteroid Belt between Jupiter and Mars. There are also comets in space, and they are made mostly from rock and ice. As one approaches the sun, its ice begins to melt. Water vapor and rock particles stream off, forming the comet's bright tail. Both comets and asteroids are thought to contain more iridium than is found on the surface of the earth.

At first Luis thought that asteroids crash into the earth more often than comets do. So here is what he proposed:

When the asteroid hit, it exploded into millions of tiny pieces that were blown back into the sky along with millions of tons of dust and rock from the earth. The dust formed a huge cloud that swirled around the planet, blocking out sunlight for several months. Darkness and sudden changes in temperature made it a difficult place in which to live. Without sunlight, plants wilted and died. Once that happened, the dinosaurs were doomed. First the plant-eating dinosaurs ran out of food. When they died, the meat-eaters had nothing to feed on, either. Slowly, they starved to death. Over the next few months, as the dust cloud settled to earth, it formed a thin layer of clay—the very same layer that Walter found in the gorge behind Gubbio millions of years later.

If Luis's ideas are correct, the world of dinosaurs ended abruptly—in a cosmic calamity. But although they are gone, the dinosaurs did not vanish without a trace. They left clues for us to find, buried deep in the rocks beneath our feet.

Metoposaurus skeleton

As a pond dried up, these animals died and became fossilized together.

Discovering Dinosaurs

Until 160 years ago, no one even knew dinosaurs had been here. Then one spring morning in 1822, an English doctor named Gideon Mantell set off to visit a sick patient. Because it was such a fine day, his wife Mary went along for the ride. While she waited for him, Mrs. Mantell wandered along a little country lane. Suddenly, in a pile of rubble, she noticed a strange rock glinting in the sunlight. She picked it up and discovered it was a fossil. Fossils are the remains of animals or plants that have been buried in the ground for millions of years and have turned to stone.

Mary Mantell

Mrs. Mantell knew her husband liked rocks, especially fossils. In fact, she sometimes thought that he liked them better than anything else. Their house was so filled with fossils that there was barely room for her and their children. When she showed him the fossil she had found, he was pleased and excited. He knew it was a tooth, but he had never seen one like it.

Dr. Mantell learned that the rocks by the roadside had come from a stone quarry near his home in Sussex. Immediately he paid it a visit. To his great delight, he found several more teeth, some bones, and a strange animal horn. Over the next few months, he asked many fossil experts about his discoveries. They were polite, but at first none of them was very interested in what he had to show. One man felt that the horn belonged to an ancient rhinoceros. Another told him that the bones and teeth had come from a hippopotamus. Dr. Mantell thought both were wrong. Mammal remains were never found in those particular rocks.

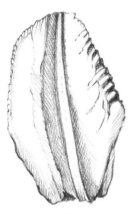

Iguanadon tooth

Finally, Mantell realized the fossil teeth were just like the teeth of iguana lizards, except that they were ten times as big. Other experts quickly agreed the teeth had belonged to a gigantic reptile that ate plants. Dr. Mantell named the creature *Iguanodon*—"iguana tooth." He drew a picture of a giant lizard with a rhinolike horn on its nose, to show what it looked like.

Over the next twenty years, many more giant bones were found in Europe, and fossil hunters wondered what to call these strange creatures. Then, in 1841, another Englishman, Richard Owen, invented the word "dinosaur," which means "terrible lizard." Owen worked at the London Zoo, examining dead animals to find out why they had died. It may sound like a horrible job, but Owen learned a lot about the way animals are built. Even so, he made some wrong guesses about dinosaurs.

In 1852 a new park was to be built next to the Crystal Palace, just outside London. Queen Victoria's husband, Prince Albert, wanted life-size replicas of dinosaurs and other beasts from long ago placed on the grounds. Richard Owen was asked to build them and he engaged a sculptor named Waterhouse Hawkins to help. As construction progressed, their workshop presented a truly amazing sight. Concrete and scaffolding and pieces of partly built monsters littered the floor. *Iguanodon* grew so large that Owen and Hawkins were able to hold a dinner party for twenty guests within its half-finished frame.

When Victoria and Albert opened the park, forty thousand people turned out to cheer. *Iguanodon* looked just like a giant lizard creeping through the bushes on all fours. Proudly displayed on the end of its nose was its horn. Everyone agreed that the exhibit was a great success. Yet only a few years were to pass before a dramatic discovery showed that many of Owen's ideas about dinosaurs were wrong.

17   In 1878 the skeletons of not one but a whole herd of *Iguanodon*s were discovered in a Belgian coal mine. From these bones it was clear that *Iguanodon* walked on two legs, not on all fours. The "horn" was part of the creature's hand and did not belong on its head at all. *Iguanodon* used it as a spike to fight off its enemies. It was obvious there was still a lot to be learned about the dinosaurs. By now, the search had shifted to America, where hillsides filled with bones were waiting to be found.

Iguanadons

The Giants Emerge

Hadrosaurus

While people in Europe were celebrating the arrival of the dinosaurs outside the Crystal Palace, Americans were beginning to puzzle over the dinosaurs, too. The first hint of dinosaur fossils in America came in 1854 when handfuls of large teeth were found near the Judith River, in what is now Montana. No bones were discovered, and everyone waited eagerly to see what the rest of the creature was like. A few years later, the wish came true when similar teeth and some giant bones were dug out of muddy limestone in New Jersey. Yet when the bones were put together, no one knew what to think. The creature was clearly a dinosaur, but it looked nothing like any dinosaur found so far.

The animal's shape was very odd. Its arms were much shorter than its legs. The creature was about twenty-five feet long, and when it stood up on its hind legs its bottom was a clear six feet above the ground. At first, it reminded scientists of a kangaroo. They decided that, like a kangaroo, it hopped. A few years later, scientists changed their minds. As more bones were found, they realized it was a distant cousin of the *Iguanodon* and probably walked in a more dignified manner on its hind feet.

The hadrosaurs, as these creatures were called, had rows of hundreds of teeth that were good at grinding the tough plants they ate. Over the years many more of their skeletons were found, and scientists realized hadrosaurs were very common toward the end of the time of the dinosaurs. Besides their teeth, their most peculiar features were their webbed feet and long, flat snouts. They were nicknamed "duck-billed dinosaurs."

19   By now, many fossil hunters knew about the dinosaurs. The race was on to find the best and the biggest bones. The two most famous dinosaur hunters in America were Edward Drinker Cope and Othniel Charles Marsh. Both were stubborn men, and Cope had a fiery temper. They hated each other, fighting viciously in a race to unearth the ancient beasts. Their feud had a good side, though. In the 1860s, when the two men started looking for dinosaur bones, only nine kinds of dinosaurs were known. By the end of the century, when both men were dead, 136 new kinds had been found.

Cope

The two men were never good friends, but the fight began in earnest when Marsh paid Cope a visit in 1870. Cope had discovered the skeleton of a remarkable animal with a long, thin neck. He called it *Elasmosaurus*—the "ribbon reptile." When Marsh saw the skeleton he knew at once why the neck was so slender. Cope had built the animal backward and had put the head on the end of the tail! It wasn't a new kind of dinosaur at all, Marsh said. It was a marine reptile, a plesiosaur.

Cope was furious with himself. He was even more annoyed that Marsh had pointed out his mistake. Cope had just written an article about the elasmosaur, but now it was all wrong. He tried to destroy all the copies of the article. Just to be mean, Marsh kept the two he had. The men were enemies from that day on.

Marsh

The most exciting dinosaurs Marsh and Cope discovered were the gigantic sauropods, the largest dinosaurs of all. Some of them, like *Brontosaurus* and *Diplodocus,* were so tall that if they were alive today they could peek in the top window of a four-story building. They had tiny heads, short bodies, and long tails like whips. But what were these creatures like? How did they live? Marsh and Cope argued about them a hundred years ago, and scientists still argue about them today.

One early mystery concerned the shape of *Diplodocus,* a sauropod Marsh first found in the western United States. *Diplodocus* was ninety feet in length—thirty feet longer than any dinosaur found so far. There were seventy-three bones in its tail alone. *Diplodocus* quickly became the favorite dinosaur of Andrew Carnegie, a millionaire. He paid dinosaur hunters to search for a complete skeleton of *Diplodocus.* When one was found, it was named *Diplodocus carnegiei* in his honor.

Carnegie opened a museum in Pittsburgh, where the skeleton of *Diplodocus* was put on display. King Edward VII of England came to visit and liked *Diplodocus* so much that Andrew Carnegie had a life-size copy of it made for him. It was shipped to London so the king could see the dinosaur any time he chose. Carnegie sent other copies to the king of Germany and to many museums around the world.

Unfortunately there were problems with the gifts. In Pittsburgh, *Diplodocus* had been put together with its legs close to its body, to support its great weight. Many experts in Europe argued with this. *Diplodocus* should look like other reptiles, they said. It should have bent legs like an alligator's.

Walter Holland, who was in charge of the Carnegie Museum, refused to change his mind. When he was shown a picture of *Diplodocus* with its legs bent, he just shook his head. *Diplodocus* looked pretty silly that way, he thought. It was short and clumsy, and worst of all, its joints were horribly out of place. The poor dinosaur would have been in constant pain. Besides, Holland pointed out, *Diplodocus* had a deep body and long ribs. If its legs had been bent, its belly would have scraped along the ground. It would have needed a rut to walk in!

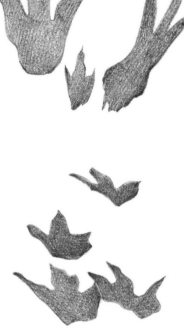

In 1938, proof was found that Holland was right. In Glen Rose, Texas, a man named Roland T. Bird found dinosaur tracks preserved in an old riverbed. They had been left in the mud 100 million years earlier by another huge sauropod, a brontosaur. When Bird measured the footprints, he found that the brontosaur's stride was twelve feet long. The distance between its left and right legs was six feet. If these creatures' legs were spread out like an alligator's, their feet would have been much farther apart.

Even if the sauropods stood upright, their great size was still a puzzle. How did they support their weight? Today the largest animals are the whales, and they live in the sea. Perhaps the sauropods lived in the water, too, reasoned some scientists. Perhaps they stood on the firm bottoms of lakes and used their long necks as snorkels. Then only their heads would have poked above the water so they could breathe.

This seemed a good idea, and it received a boost when Roland T. Bird found more sauropod tracks. This time they were made by a *swimming* dinosaur. The tracks showed only the dinosaur's front feet, as it kicked the bottom to push itself along. Its heavy tail and back feet were floating in the water. Then, there was the single print of a back foot as the dinosaur suddenly turned and kicked off in a new direction.

Dinosaur tracks

It was not until 1951 that an English scientist, Kenneth Kermack, figured out why the idea was wrong. If a sauropod stood in water twenty feet deep, the pressure would be so great it would crush the dinosaur's neck. What was more, the animal's lungs could not expand and contract, so the animal would not be able to breathe. As the water pressed in from all sides, *Diplodocus* would have been squeezed to death. But everyone ignored these arguments, and the sauropods were left in the water for the next twenty years.

In 1971, the creatures were finally rescued and put on dry land by a young scientist named Robert Bakker, who was studying at Yale. When he compared sauropod fossils to bones of two animals alive today, the whole idea of water-living sauropods fell apart. Hippopotamuses, for example, live in water, and they have wide, flat bodies. Elephants, on the other hand, live on land, and their bodies are thinner and deeper. The sauropods' bodies were much more like those of elephants. So, Bakker said, they probably lived on land, too.

Bakker suggested that sauropods even ate like elephants. Elephants use their trunks to tear leaves and branches from trees. By rearing up on their hind legs and using their tails for balance, the sauropods could reach the treetops, too. If they were attacked, the sauropods would bring their big front feet down with a crash. It is no wonder that *Brontosaurus* means "thunder lizard." Even the fiercest flesh-eating dinosaur would not like to be stomped by a brontosaur's foot.

Each time a new dinosaur is discovered, a new set of puzzles has to be solved. And as the next chapter shows, scientists rarely agree for long as to which answer is correct.

Dinosaur Puzzles

One day in 1979, visitors to the Carnegie Museum in Pittsburgh came across an unexpected sight. Workmen were putting up ladders next to the *Brontosaurus* skeleton. Then they climbed up, sawed off the brontosaur's head, and carefully attached a new one in its place. The same thing happened in museums all over America. Why? Because scientists had just realized that *Brontosaurus* had been wearing the wrong head for the last one hundred years.

One of the very first brontosaurs was found by Othniel Marsh's collectors at Como Bluff, Wyoming, in 1879. It was a beautifully preserved skeleton—except it had no head. Marsh had found a head in a nearby quarry that seemed to fit, so he stuck it on instead.

Marsh had guessed, but he guessed wrong. In 1909, a more complete brontosaur was found in Jensen, Utah, and this time it had a head. It was quite unlike the one Marsh had used, being long and slender rather than short and fat. Eventually, it was realized that these long-necked dinosaurs came in two separate groups. And while *Brontosaurus*'s body belongs to one group, the first head it had been given belongs to the other. Now museums are quietly correcting the mistake.

Putting dinosaurs together is a risky business. When you look at the giant bones of dinosaurs in museums, it may seem like a lot is known about them. But this is not always true. Scientists who find the bones have to piece them together, like an enormous jigsaw puzzle. A dinosaur hunter once said, "I find little bits of dinosaurs and just try to make bigger bits out of them."

When only fragments of a skeleton are found, everyone

23

Brontosaurus bones

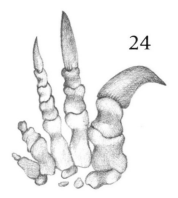

24

is left pondering what the rest of the creature was like. A few years ago a Polish expedition to Asia found a pair of dinosaur hands three feet long. They were attached to arms that stretched the length of a small car. This creature, what little there is of it, is named *Deinocheirus*, "terrible hand." Was *Deinocheirus* a ferocious meat-eater, even more terrifying than *Tyrannosaurus rex*? Or did it use its huge arms for hanging upside down like a giant sloth? So far, no one can tell.

Sometimes scientists can piece together bones from different skeletons to make a complete dinosaur. That is how we learned about *Tyrannosaurus*. A single, entire skeleton has never been found.

Because of its huge jaws, filled with dozens of curved, jagged teeth up to six inches in length, *Tyrannosaurus* has a reputation as the greatest hunter of all. But this may not be correct. When Barney Newman, a scientist at the British Museum in London, examined their tyrannosaur, he realized its legs could not move back and forth very far. The giant monster may have taken mincing steps. Newman decided it could walk only slowly, about as fast as a man. With its thick tail swinging behind it, *Tyrannosaurus* might have waddled like a goose! Since it could not move fast, the tyrannosaur probably waited for its prey to wander by and then jumped on it. Or it may have been a scavenger, eating animals that were already dead.

Another surprise is that *Tyrannosaurus* had arms so short they could not even reach its mouth. These stubby arms had only two small fingers, and would have been little help in catching other animals. The monster relied on its teeth and clawed feet to tear its prey apart. So what were its arms for?

Perhaps after big meals *Tyrannosaurus* became drowsy and lay down to take a nap. It stretched out its neck, rested its chin on the ground, and folded its legs beneath its body. How could it stand up again? If it straightened out its legs, its chest and head would scrape along the ground. But if it used its little arms to give itself a push, it could arch its neck backward, swinging up until it balanced on its hind legs again.

The discovery of *Stegosaurus* posed a different kind of problem. Scientists did not understand how some parts of the creature fitted together. Imagine you uncover a skeleton of a plant-eating dinosaur. All the usual bones, such as ribs and legs and feet, are there. But as you keep digging, you find a head so small that it is hard to believe it could belong to this bulky animal. Finally you come across lots of flat, pointed plates and four spikes, each one three feet long. What are the plates for? Where on the animal do they belong?

Scientists tried many ways to arrange the mysterious plates. Some thought they were armor and stood up in rows along the dinosaur's back. One expert pointed out that this would not protect *Stegosaurus* very well. He suggested the plates lay flat instead. This gave *Stegosaurus* an unhappy, floppy look. Perhaps a better idea, suggested by other scientists, is that the plates kept the stegosaur cool. The plates were filled with blood vessels. When the animal got too hot, blood pumped through the bony panels would lose heat to the surrounding air. Elephants use their big ears to keep cool in this way today.

To find out how good the plates really were at losing heat, James Farlow and some other scientists built a model stegosaur and put it in a wind tunnel. Wind tunnels are used to test how wind effects all kinds of things, such as airplanes. The scientists heated up the stegosaur model, blew wind over it, and then waited for it to cool. They tried the experiment several times, arranging the plates in different ways. When the plates were lined up in two rows standing side by side, the model cooled down fastest. This may be how the plates were arranged on a real stegosaur.

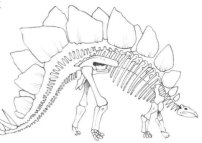

Stegosaurus

Once scientists agree what a dinosaur looked like, they can figure out roughly how much it weighed. Dinosaurs' flesh is almost never found, but their bones have scars on them where muscles were attached. From these, experts can guess how big the muscles were and how they were arranged. Then they make a small model of the dinosaur and put it into a tank filled with water. The model pushes away, or displaces, the same amount of water as it takes up itself. The amount of water pushed away is measured and a formula is used to find out how much the dinosaur weighed.

The first time people tried to figure out dinosaur weights, there were some surprises. *Stegosaurus,* which looked quite big, weighed less than two tons. *Tyrannosaurus* weighed seven tons, more than a fully grown African elephant. *Diplodocus* looked as if it weighed thirty tons, but turned out to weigh only ten. Enormous *Brachiosaurus* gained weight, from fifty to eighty tons, the weight of more than ten elephants.

Scientists change their minds about dinosaurs so often because little is known of these magnificent beasts. As they argue, they hope to edge closer to the truth. Mostly the disputes are about small details, but, as we shall see, occasionally they are about much bigger ideas.

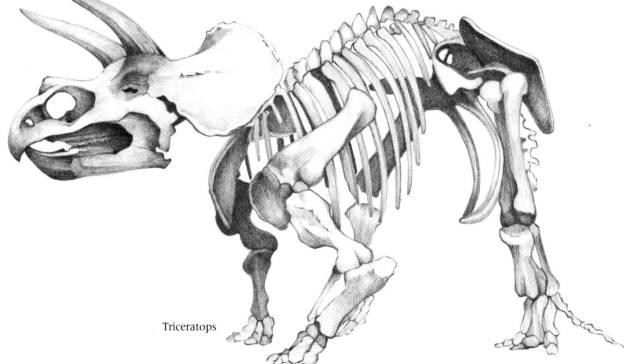

Triceratops

Hot-Blooded Dinosaurs

Scientists are certain the last dinosaur died millions of years ago, but every so often people claim they have seen strange dinosaurlike monsters lurking about. The most famous one is Nessie, who is supposed to live in the chilly waters of Loch Ness, in Scotland. Dozens of visitors to the lake say they have seen her. Some have even taken blurry photographs that show a head and a long, slender neck poking out of the water. Could Nessie be a creature left over from the past? Is she a plesiosaur, one of the giant marine reptiles that swam in the seas when dinosaurs stalked the land?

Sadly, most scientists think not. No one has ever found bones or other traces of such a creature as Nessie. Scientists think the strange-looking objects in photographs are probably patches of plants floating in the water. Or perhaps they are remains of tree trunks that filled with gas as they rotted, and bobbed to the surface from the depths of the lake.

Still, what *would* happen if a living dinosaur were found? The very first thing scientists might do is take its temperature. This would settle once and for all a fierce argument that has been raging for the past few years: Were dinosaurs hot-blooded or cold-blooded? It would be useful to know because it would tell us a great deal about what dinosaurs were like.

When the dinosaurs were first discovered, they were assumed to be cold-blooded like their reptile cousins, the lizards, crocodiles, and snakes. These animals are not usually very active or very smart, and so dinosaurs were pictured as slow-moving, dim-witted giants who led rather quiet

Mosasaurs

27

lives. Recently, some scientists have claimed that dinosaurs were hot-blooded like mammals and birds. Some dinosaurs, they now think, were very active and agile, and intelligent, too. Before seeing why these scientists have changed their minds, let's see what it means to be hot-blooded or cold-blooded.

If you hold a lizard in your hand it doesn't feel cold, but it isn't very warm, either. A reptile's body produces little heat of its own, which is why it is called cold-blooded. Also, a reptile's body is covered with scales rather than feathers or fur, so it cannot keep itself warm. Its temperature is always close to that of its surroundings. This is why most reptiles live in the tropics or in deserts; you would never find a reptile near the North Pole. When a reptile gets cold, it simply slows down.

Even when they are nice and warm, reptiles cannot stay active for very long. Most have hearts that do not pump blood or oxygen around their bodies very well. This limits the supply of oxygen to their muscles. A lizard can move fairly rapidly when it has to (as anyone who has tried to catch one knows), but it quickly runs out of breath. Reptiles spend their time scuttling back and forth between sun and shade, lying in wait for their prey.

Birds and mammals are called hot-blooded because they can keep their bodies warm. They can stay active in cold weather and hot, and they have special ways of keeping their temperatures just right. We humans perspire when we get too hot. As the sweat on our skin evaporates, it cools us down. When we get cold we shiver, which helps our muscles to produce more heat. Some furry mammals, like dogs, do not sweat (except through the pads on their feet), but pant instead. Snakes cannot shiver, and crocodiles cannot sweat. Could the dinosaurs? Were they hot-blooded, too?

Modern cold-blooded animals

John Ostrom was one of the first scientists to suggest they were. He works at the Peabody Museum at Yale, where he looks after all the dinosaur bones Othniel Marsh collected a hundred years ago. In the summer he often leaves the museum and heads for Wyoming or Montana to search for new kinds of dinosaurs. Often it takes weeks to scour the barren hillsides where fossil-bearing rocks have been exposed. Dinosaur hunting is not always as much fun as it sounds.

One day in 1964, as he was packing to go back to Yale, John Ostrom discovered the most exciting dinosaur he had ever seen. To most people it might not seem so special, but the creature that emerged from the rocks in the final days of that summer changed forever Ostrom's ideas about how dinosaurs had lived.

The new dinosaur was small and lightly built. When it stood on its back legs, it was six feet tall and measured fourteen feet from its head to the tip of its tail. It was not much larger than a man. Two odd features caught Ostrom's attention. To begin with, the bones of its tail were fused together, making the tail stick out straight like a long, flexible pole. There was something even stranger. The creature's weapons, two huge, curved claws, were on its *back* feet. How could it capture its prey—for this was a meat-eating dinosaur—with its weapons attached to its toes?

Ostrom noticed that these clawed toes, one on each foot, could be bent back much farther than the other toes. Suddenly it made sense. When this dinosaur chased its prey, it delicately lifted the claws away from the ground. It attacked feet first, jumping on its victim, slashing ferociously with its savage weapons. The rigid tail acted like a tightrope walker's pole, helping the dinosaur to keep its balance until its prey was dead. I would not like to meet this creature on a dark night, Ostrom thought. He named the animal *Deinonychus*, which means "terrible claw."

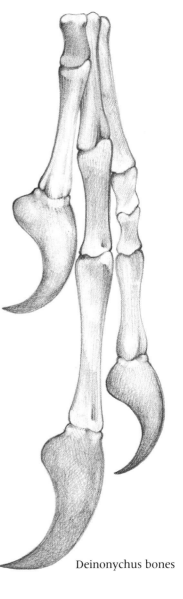

Deinonychus bones

Deinonychus

As Ostrom's vision of *Deinonychus* took shape, he began to realize how agile and fast moving the creature must have been. His dinosaur did not fit the old picture of slow, sluggish dinosaurs. If dinosaurs were very active, Ostrom wondered, were they hot-blooded, too?

A few years later, John Ostrom made another astonishing discovery. He was in a tiny Dutch museum, studying the fossil of a pterosaur, a flying reptile that lived alongside the dinosaurs. He realized something was wrong. The bones were much too heavy for a pterosaur. They looked more like those of a small meat-eating dinosaur. He caught sight of something no one had noticed before: Faint, but unmistakable impressions of feathers were etched in the rock. It was neither a pterosaur nor a dinosaur. It was *Archaeopteryx*, the very first bird! These fossils are very rare. Only four of them had ever been found, and one was just the imprint of a single feather. Ostrom was very excited indeed.

He had another idea. The fossil *looked* like a dinosaur, but the feathers told him it was a bird. After careful study, he decided that dinosaurs and birds were close relatives. In fact, birds were descended from dinosaurs. This was the link he had been searching for. Birds had inherited their hot-bloodedness from their ancestors, the hot-blooded dinosaurs.

Meanwhile, other scientists were finding more clues.

Robert Bakker, who had been a student of Ostrom's, pointed out that many dinosaurs simply look as though they were built for speed. *Ornithomimus*, for example, was an elegant dinosaur with long, slim legs. It looked very much like an ostrich, a flightless bird that can run fifty miles per hour or more. It made no sense, Bakker said, to suppose that *Ornithomimus* was a cold-blooded creature that could not move very fast.

Bakker had a second idea, perhaps the most clever of all. Birds and mammals need a lot of food to produce the heat that keeps them warm. In fact, hot-blooded animals eat ten

Seabird feather

times as much food as cold-blooded ones. A lion in a zoo must be fed every day, while a crocodile or snake lives nicely if it eats one meal every two or three weeks. How much, Bakker wondered, did dinosaurs eat? You might think it an impossible question to answer, but he thought of a way to find out.

Bakker began visiting many museums to count different kinds of dinosaurs. First he counted the predators, the meat-eating dinosaurs, then he counted their prey, the plant-eaters. If dinosaurs were cold-blooded, the predators would not have to eat very often. A lot of predators could live off quite a small number of prey animals. If dinosaurs were hot-blooded, and ate more often, there would be many fewer predatory, or meat-eating, ones. Everywhere Bakker looked, that is exactly what he found. The bones of the plant-eaters are plentiful, but bones of meat-eating ones are very rare. This suggested that some dinosaurs had hearty, hot-blooded appetites.

Scientists are still arguing about these ideas, but the thought of fast, active dinosaurs does make a lot of sense. If the dinosaurs were as energetic as Ostrom and Bakker suggest, it is easy to understand how they took over the earth and successfully ruled it for so long.

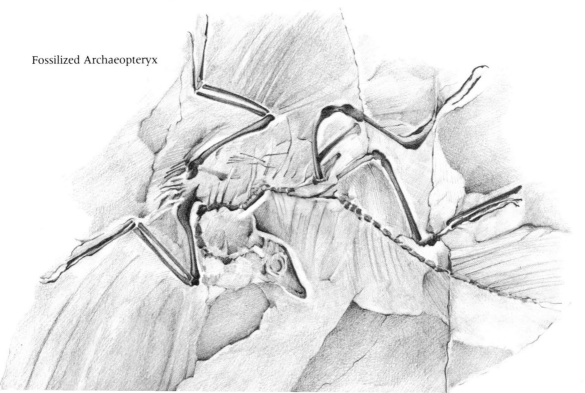

Fossilized Archaeopteryx

And Then There Were None

Sometimes it seems as if there are as many ideas about what caused the dinosaurs to die out as there were kinds of dinosaurs. And just like the dinosaurs themselves, some of these ideas seem sensible and some seem silly when we look at them.

Flowering plants first appeared in the middle of the dinosaurs' time, gracing the countryside with cheerful splashes of color. Could they have killed the dinosaurs? Some scientists think so, because the lovely blossoms had a darker side. Some flowers contained chemicals the dinosaurs were not used to eating. If the dinosaurs' sense of taste was not sharp enough to tell them that the plants were poisonous, they may have eaten them by mistake.

If the dinosaurs were not poisoned, they may have suffered another fate. Flowers lack the oily substances found in ferns and pines. Without these oils, flowering plants might have been hard for a dinosaur to digest. Did they die of constipation?

Not many scientists take these ideas seriously. After all, flowers appeared millions of years before the dinosaurs came to an end. Herds of hadrosaurs and other plant-eaters roamed the plains quite happily. The flowers surrounding them don't seem to have done them much harm.

Other scientists think the dinosaurs perished because they could not adjust to changes in the earth's climate. Sometimes these changes are due to movements of the enormous plates that form our planet's surface. Over millions of years, the continents move toward each other or drift apart. When continents meet, mountains are built as the force of the collision folds the land and piles it high. During the age of dinosaurs, the levels of the seas rose when a large plate, which stretched to the South Pole, split apart. Shallow seas spread over much of the land, and the climate was pleasant and warm. In the middle of the time of the dinosaurs, the continents continued to break up into smaller chunks of land. As the continents moved, the climate changed. Summers became hotter, and winters grew colder. Dinosaurs might have found it hard to cope.

Even the first mammals, our shrewlike ancestors, have been blamed. Some scientists say they were getting too smart. They prowled at night while the dinosaurs slept. Perhaps the mammals stole dinosaur eggs and gobbled them up faster than the dinosaurs could lay them. Perhaps, but these little animals probably were not much smarter than the dinosaurs next door.

There *are* some signs that there were fewer kinds of dinosaurs toward the end. But the last ones to roam the earth seem to have been as happy and healthy as the first. Where were dinosaurs headed when they disappeared? In the last few years, scientists have found clues that some dinosaurs were pretty smart. Strange though it may seem, in some ways the dinosaurs were becoming more like people.

In 1978, John Horner, a young paleontologist from Princeton University, made an unusual discovery. In Glacier National Park, on the banks of an old riverbed, he found a dinosaur nursery. There were several bowl-shaped nests, each one about ten feet across and made from mud. Inside the nests were fossil eggs, along with skeletons of newly hatched babies and of several older nestlings four or five feet long. The nests had been built by maiasaurs, a kind of duck-billed dinosaur. These placid plant-eating creatures were very common toward the end of the age of dinosaurs.

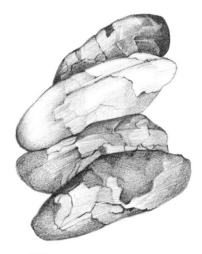

When Horner examined the little skeletons he found that the babies' teeth were quite worn. The young dinosaurs had

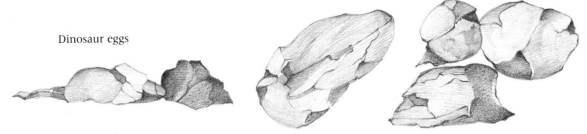

Dinosaur eggs

been eating coarse leaves and plants for some time. Since they were still in their nests, Horner realized their parents must have brought them food and cared for them for many months after they hatched. So it seems dinosaurs, like us, had a family life.

These discoveries came as a great surprise. They suggested that dinosaurs were smarter than scientists had thought. Among today's animals, it is mostly the intelligent ones, such as mammals and birds, that look after their young. Of the reptiles, only crocodiles guard their nests and take care of their babies after they hatch. Snakes and lizards simply lay eggs and leave their children to fend for themselves. So how smart were the dinosaurs? One way to find out is to look at the sizes of their brains.

Originally, dinosaurs were thought to be dumb because their brains were too small for their bodies. Now most scientists agree this was a mistake. Larger animals *always* have relatively smaller brains than littler ones, but this does not mean they are any less smart. What happens is that as bodies get bigger so do brains, but brains do not increase in size as fast. When scientists want to compare them, they divide the weight of an animal's brain by the weight of its body. When this was done for different kinds of dinosaurs, the results were very interesting.

Brontosaurs and other giant sauropods came off worst. They probably *weren't* very smart. Since they were so huge, with few enemies, perhaps they did not need to be smart. Next came the armored dinosaurs like *Stegosaurus,* and the horned dinosaurs like *Triceratops.* The duckbills like *Maiasaurus,* with their beginnings of family life, were the brainiest plant-eating dinosaurs. Meat-eating tyrannosaurs were more clever still. They had to be: It takes more intelligence to catch your dinner on the move than it does to munch on a plant. And, as far as we know, a strange little creature called *Stenonychosaurus* was the smartest of all.

The first *Stenonychosaurus* was found in Alberta by Dale Russell, who works for the National Museum of Canada. It was a lightly built meat-eater that could run very fast. It had delicate hands with movable thumbs much like our own, and two large forward-facing eyes. Like us, it probably could see in three dimensions. It was an unusual reptile. Sixty-five million years ago, it may have been the most intelligent creature that had ever lived on earth.

Stenonychosaurus evolved late in the age of the dinosaurs. Just as they were becoming clever, they were gone. Given luck, Russell says, and a lot more time, they might even have produced a kind of dinosaur-man.

We humans owe a lot to the disappearance of the dinosaurs. After they vanished, our mammal ancestors, many no larger than shrews, quickly took over the earth. The scene was set for the arrival of wallabies and whales, bats and bears, and, eventually, us.

Could whatever happened when the dinosaurs died happen again? Some scientists think so—which brings us back to the thin ribbon of clay that Walter Alvarez found. Sixty-five million years ago, *something* happened to make that clay layer form. So far, the best guess is that an asteroid or comet was flying through space, and the earth was in the way.

The Meeting in Snowbird

Not long ago, scientists from all over the world gathered in Snowbird, Utah, to talk. Some of them were experts on asteroids and comets. Others were interested in dinosaurs. All of them had two questions in mind. If Luis Alvarez was right and 65 million years ago an asteroid or a comet hit the earth, where did it land? And if it did land, did it kill the dinosaurs?

Some scientists wanted to show that the idea was wrong. Others were convinced that it was right. They brought lots of arguments to persuade their fellow scientists one way or the other.

Everyone agreed that there are plenty of asteroids flying in space. About forty thousand of them are clustered together in the Asteroid Belt, a region of space between Jupiter and Mars. Most of the time, these asteroids are well behaved. Like tiny planets, they circle the sun. Then, every so often, something goes wrong. An asteroid is thrown out of orbit by Jupiter's great gravitational field. The asteroid heads off on its own, sometimes on a path that may cross that of the earth.

Comets are born much farther from the sun. Millions of these huge, lumpy snowballs made of ice and rock spin in space, far past the last planet. They form a thin fringe, like a halo, around the edges of the solar system. This fringe is known as the Oort Cloud. Astronomers believe it is debris left over from the formation of the solar system, four and a half billion years ago. Sometimes a distant star disturbs the Oort Cloud and sends a comet hurtling toward the sun. As it does, part of it begins to melt. The comet's head becomes fuzzy as bits of ice and rock stream off to form a long, glowing tail that trails behind it across the sky.

For a long time, no one realized that rocky bodies from space could strike the earth and change its history. But when spacecraft started photographing our moon and the other planets, scientists saw that almost all are scarred by craters. The face that smiles back when we look at the moon is composed of craters, proving that the moon was visited by asteroids and comets long ago.

The surface of Mercury is covered with craters, too. It has been hit so often there is barely an inch to spare between holes. Recently, scientists photographed an even more astonishing sight. Mimas, one of Saturn's moons, has a crater so big it covers almost one side!

Craters on earth are much harder to see. Wind and rain and the earth's active geology quickly wear away the scars. Even so, scientists at Snowbird were told, more than one hundred craters have been found. One of the best preserved is Meteor Crater, near Flagstaff, Arizona. That hole is a mile wide and six hundred feet deep. It formed twenty-five thousand years ago, when a small asteroid crashed into the earth. The Apollo astronauts were trained there so they would feel at home when they went to the moon.

Luis Alvarez explained that if an asteroid landed 65 million years ago, it would have made a much larger crater, one about a hundred miles wide. Three craters of about this size have been found—Vredefort in South Africa, Sudbury in Canada, and Popigai in the Soviet Union. Unfortunately, none of them is the right age. The first two were formed nearly 2 billion years ago. Popigai is only 40 million years old. It was created 25 million years after the last dinosaur disappeared. So where *did* the asteroid or comet land?

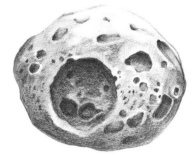

Some scientists suggested it may have landed in the sea. If that had happened, a great crater would have been formed. By today it would have vanished, covered by mud and rocks and destroyed by movements of the sea floor.

Another question the Snowbird scientists tried to answer is how much energy would be released by a collision of the earth with an asteroid or a comet. This would tell them whether an explosion could send the dust high into the atmosphere. This dust would affect the plants and animals on the ground. To help everyone understand, the scientists showed pictures of the biggest explosions we know about—nuclear bombs. It turns out that blasts from nuclear bombs might be a lot like what happens when a body from space hits the earth.

Let's try to imagine what the crash would be like. Imagine that a huge rock, six miles wide and traveling at eighteen thousand miles per hour, collides with the earth with the force of a thousand billion tons of dynamite. In a blinding flash, it turns into a boiling ball of molten metal and rock. It bores down into the earth for several miles like a gigantic drill. Within a fraction of a second, shock waves shudder through the earth, moving faster than the speed of sound. Close to the impact, minerals are turned instantly into glass, and rocks are smashed and hurled into the air for a hundred miles around. An enormous black cloud of vaporized particles and melted matter billows into the sky. Beneath the cloud is a crater five miles deep. Its glistening floor churns with white-hot, liquid rock.

What happens next can only be guessed, but here is what Walter and Luis Alvarez think. The cloud of dust sweeps around the earth, a thick, swirling mass that hovers overhead for months. So little sunlight fights through that even the days seem like night. Without light, plants stop growing. The dinosaurs and other animals stumble around in the dark and soon can find nothing to eat.

The scientists heard that other things might have happened, too. Without the sun's rays to warm it, the air would quickly cool. Temperatures would plunge below zero, and the dinosaurs would freeze. If the object landed in the ocean,

39 great waves would sweep through the seas. Waves nearly
    a mile high would flood the land. No signs of a great flood
    have been found.

    After Snowbird, the questions remained. Did an asteroid
    or comet hit the earth? Did the dinosaurs freeze, or did they
    starve or drown? But before long, within little more than a
    year, some very curious answers began to emerge.

The Dark Star and Us

When you look at the sky on a clear, dark night, you see the tiny flickering lights of distant stars. Sometimes a faint streak of light will trace the faraway journey of a meteor or "shooting star" in its fiery, final moment of glory. Now imagine the sky ablaze with the brilliant light of many comets—so many that you cannot count them all. No one has ever seen such a sight, yet that is where the mystery has finally led. If some scientists are right, every so often a billion comets sweep through our solar system! Each comet shower lasts a million years or more, and before it ends, two dozen of the huge icy bodies may have struck the earth.

This latest twist to the tale turned up when David Raup and John Sepkoski, two scientists at the University of Chicago, looked at the fossil records of marine animals that had died out during the last 250 million years. They wanted to work out how many great extinctions there had been in the recent history of the earth. The fossils told them a lot about the sea creatures that lived during this time, although not much about the ones that lived before that.

Gathering all the information was painstaking work—John Sepkoski had started nearly ten years before. Finally, in the spring of 1983, they drew a line from one extinction to the next. To their surprise, a pattern emerged. On their drawing, the line rose sharply to a point every 28 million years. Each peak marks a mass extinction when many kinds of life died at once. In all, twelve peaks zigzagged across their paper. The peak 65 million years ago was one of the biggest. It is also the most famous by far, because afterward the dinosaurs were seen no more.

40

What did it mean? Did mass extinctions really happen every 28 million years? If so, what caused them?

The two scientists tried and tried to think of a way to explain the pattern. They couldn't think of anything that happens on earth every 28 million years. At last, they suggested that the answer must lie outside the earth, in our solar system or in our galaxy or beyond.

Back in Berkeley, Richard Muller, a young physicist who works with Luis, heard about Raup and Sepkoski's results. They interested him, and he spent the next few weeks thinking hard. Whenever he had a new idea he discussed it with Luis Alvarez. Each time, one of them found a reason why it would not work, and Rich had to think some more. It was an exciting, frustrating time—just as thinking about the clay layer had been for Luis four years earlier. Finally, Rich came up with an idea that might solve the puzzle.

What if the sun has a companion, a small sister star that travels with her on the journey through the Milky Way? Many stars exist in pairs, and astronomers have wondered why our sun is alone. Rich liked the idea of a companion so much that he named the mystery star Nemesis, after the Greek goddess of vengeance. He and some other scientists made up a story to explain how the mystery star affects life on earth.

Nemesis formed with the sun, they said, four and a half billion years ago when our solar system was born. In the tumultuous events that marked the birth of the sun and the planets, Nemesis was flung far afield. Today it is a black or brown "dwarf," dimmer than the sun and only about one tenth as big. This little star follows a long, oval-shaped orbit, tied loosely to our sun by the pull of gravity.

Every 28 million years, as Nemesis travels its path through space, it moves to its point closest to the sun. This distance is still two thousand or more times further from the sun than the earth is. But, still, when Nemesis reaches this point, it is close enough so that the pull of its gravity stirs up the comets in the Oort Cloud, far past the last planet.

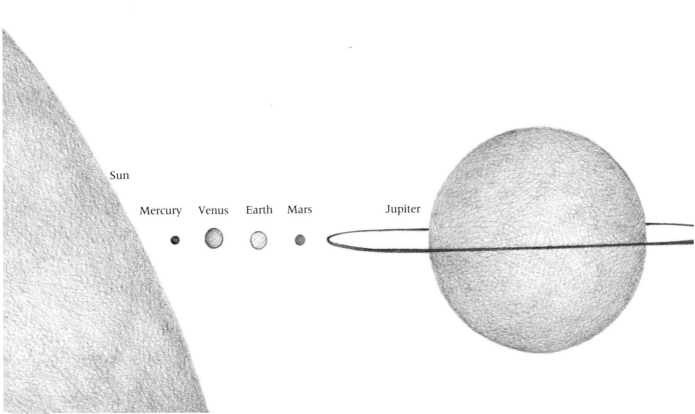

Sun

Mercury   Venus   Earth   Mars   Jupiter

A billion of these comets could be jarred from the cloud and launched on wild trips through the solar system. Some of them pass close to the earth, lighting the sky so brightly that night seems like day. Then, one day, one of them hits the earth in a terrible blinding flash. Dust and rock billow high into the atmosphere, and sunlight is blocked from the earth. The creatures on the planet know darkness and cold. But hidden from sight, high above the earth, the comet shower goes on.

Not everyone believes this story, and a lot more must be learned to show whether the idea is right. But one bit of evidence has convinced some scientists that part of the tale is true.

About eighty-eight craters on the earth have been studied, and their ages determined. This is not many craters, but Richard Muller and Walter Alvarez decided to look at them to see whether they formed in cycles, too. To their delight, the scientists saw a pattern. The craters were formed in cycles. What's more, the cycles seem to match the times when mass extinctions occurred.

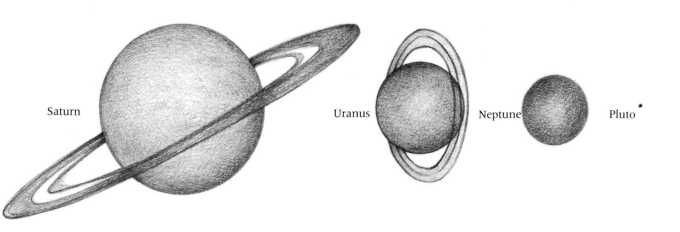

Saturn   Uranus   Neptune   Pluto

Two other scientists, Michael Rampino and Dick Stothers, also found a pattern in the craters, but suggest another cause. They say that the comet showers began when the solar system passed through the Milky Way, our galaxy.

The Milky Way resembles a frisbee or saucer in shape. Every 34 million years or so, the solar system travels from near the top of the galaxy toward the bottom. Then it travels back up again. Each time it goes through the middle of the galaxy, it may encounter huge, invisible clouds of dust and gas. The scientists say that the dust clouds' gravity disrupts the Oort Cloud, sending comets hurtling toward the sun.

Still others are drawn to the idea of Nemesis, the sun's sister star, but doubts trouble them. They worry that the chance that Nemesis is still there—if it ever was—is just too small. They think that by now it would have been drawn away from the sun, lured by the gravity of a passing star.

But what if the story is true? It is, of course, only one more idea about why the dinosaurs disappeared. But the pattern in extinctions and the matching crater ages make it seem more likely that bodies from space really do affect the creatures living here.

Even now, Rich Muller and his colleagues at Berkeley are searching the heavens for Nemesis, the dark star. They are using a special telescope that can photograph the entire sky in a few weeks. Then in a few months' time, it will photograph the sky again, and the two sets of photos will be compared by a computer. By then Nemesis will have moved slightly, and the change in its position might reveal that it is the sun's companion. Even if the little star isn't found in this search, that does not mean it isn't there. It may simply be too faint for us to see with today's telescopes. If the scientists do find the star, the dinosaur mystery may be solved at last.

As for our own future, there is no need to worry for a long time. The scientists who propose the dark star theory say that if Nemesis is there, now it is near its greatest distance from the sun. This is so far away that the star's light would take two and a half years to reach us. It will be at least 15 million years before Nemesis comes close again.

While some scientists look for the star, others are keeping an eye out for stray asteroids, looking for ones that might collide with us, just in case. Some think that by sending a rocket to space to meet it, an asteroid easily could be nudged into an orbit that would carry it away from the earth.

It's a strange tale, linking the dinosaurs and a dark star. It starts with the clay and rocks beneath our feet, and ends with our wondering eyes turned to the heavens. Studies of the dinosaurs keep leading to still more mysteries and clues. The scientists may never find the star they seek. But they are sure to find other things to learn about and question.

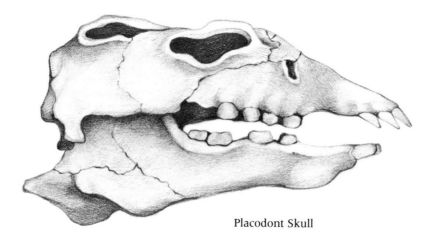

Placodont Skull

Time Line

200 million years to today

Megalosaurus

Brachiosaurus

Iguanadon

Archaeopteryx

Camarasaurus

Coelophysis

Diplodocus

Stegosaurus

Allosaurus

Deinonychus

Plateosaurus

Brontosaurus

TRIASSIC	JURASSIC	CRETACEOU
200 Million Years	195 Million Years	136 Million Years

AGE OF DINOSAURS

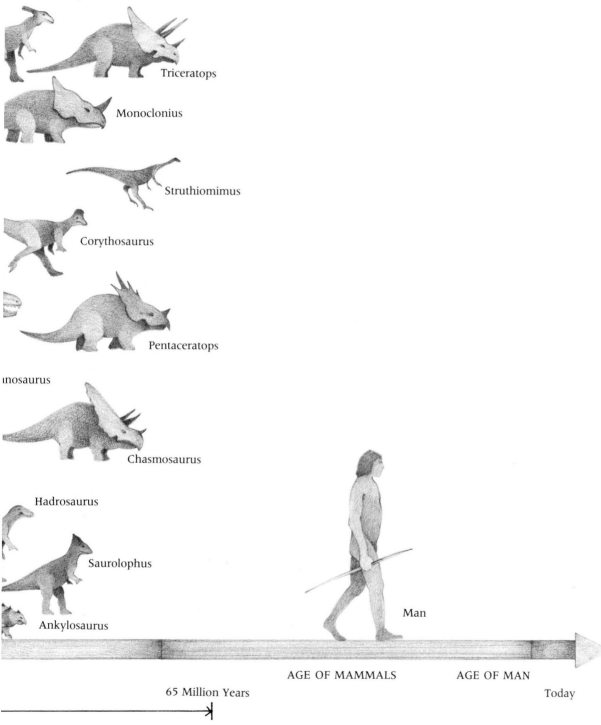

Parasaurolophus

Triceratops

Monoclonius

Struthiomimus

Corythosaurus

Pentaceratops

nosaurus

Chasmosaurus

Hadrosaurus

Saurolophus

Ankylosaurus

Man

AGE OF MAMMALS

AGE OF MAN

65 Million Years

Today

Index